# Sh'ma'

## A Concise Weekday Siddur

## For Praying in English

# Sh'ma'

## A Concise Weekday Siddur
## For Praying in English

A Selection of the Traditional Jewish Prayers

Interpreted in English by

## Rabbi Zalman Schachter-Shalomi

Edited by

N.M-Y.

Albion
Andalus
The Jewish Renewal Series
Boulder, CO
2010

*"The old shall be renewed,*

*and the new shall be made holy."*

— Rabbi Avraham Yitzhak Kook

Albion-Andalus, Inc.
P. O. Box 19852
Boulder, CO 80308
*www.albionandalus.com*

Design and composition by Albion-Andalus, Inc.
Cover design by Carlos Espinosa, Beyond 5280
Cover illustration by Netanel Miles-Yepez.

Manufactured in the United States of America

**ISBN: 1453806768**
**EAN-13: 9781453806760**

# Acknowledgements

WITH GRATITUDE TO: Netanel Miles-Yepez, who edited and adapted the translations of the *siddur* into their final form; Rabbi Ayla Grafstein, whose generosity helped make this little booklet possible; Mary Fulton, my secretary, who did much checking and formatting of previous versions of the *siddur*; the Reb Zalman Legacy Project of the Yesod Foundation and ALEPH: Alliance for Jewish Renewal, who have both done so much to make my work available to future generations; and to all the English davveners who have given me feedback over the years, this is for you.

*In loving memory of*
*Miriam bat Sarah*

# Translators Preface

Dear friend —

If you do not yet read Hebrew, and need an alternative resource for your daily *davvenen* (prayer), or if you are not used to reading the Hebrew with comprehension and the ability to dilate it from its literal meaning, I offer you this concise translation of the Jewish *siddur* or prayer-book, which I frequently use for my own *davvenen*.

I have translated the liturgy of the *siddur* here according to the way in which I experience it in my own feeling-consciousness. Thus, my translations do not so much offer the *p'shat* or the literal meaning of the words as they do a devotional interpretation that can make them into prayers of the heart.

I suggest that you *davven* it all the way through first, reading it out loud, and loud enough to hear it with feeling. Right away, you will find that you will like some sections better than others. However, you will also note that there are five distinct parts to this *siddur*, each with a different purpose.

These five parts describe the raising of awareness through the *olamot* or worlds of Jewish mysticism: from the world of *Assiyah*, where one prays the prayer of sensation, to the world of *Yetzirah*, where the prayer of feelings are offered, from there to the world of *B'riyah*, where reason and the intellect hold sway, on to the summit, the world of the *Atzilut* and intuition.

When you have finished this 'ascent' through these worlds, you will need to reflect on the 'stirrings' you may have experienced along the way and to ask yourself these questions: *How am I to apply this in my consensus reality? With my family, my friends, and the other people with whom I am in contact? How can I use this in a manner that will lead to the healing of our planet and our society?*

This is part of coming back 'down' to the grounded world of sensation and action, what is called in Hebrew, *yeridat ha'shefa'*, the 'bringing down of the Divine influx.'

If saying all of the prayers is too much for you at first, or on a particularly busy day, you may need to pick passages from each world of prayer that are most meaningful to you. Some days you may even wish to vary some parts and to say others instead, or just recite some of the sentences of blessings and proceed with your daily tasks. This *siddur* is meant to help you stay in touch with God on a daily basis, to gain divine assistance, to lighten your burdens, not to add to them.

May you come to experience your own prayer as a blessed meeting with *your own* God.

Sincerely,

Rabbi Zalman Schachter-Shalomi
Boulder, Colorado, 18 *Tishrei*,
The *yahrzeit* of Rebbe Nahman of Bratzlav

## *Modeh Ani*
### 'I Gratefully Thank You'

> As you wake up in the morning, say the (f.) *Modah/* (m.) *Modeh Ani* . . .

Thank You, Living God,
For mercifully granting
My soul another day
Of awareness;
Thank You for
This sacred trust.

## *T'fillat ha-Assiah*
### 'The Prayer of Doing'

## *Asher Yatzar*
### 'Who Formed'

> Then, in deep gratitude after using the bathroom, say *Asher Yatzar* . . .

I worship You,
*Yah*, Our God,
Cosmic Majesty;
You formed me
A human being,
So wisely;
You created in me
All manner of
Hollows and ducts,

Inner organs and
intestines.

As I am completely
Transparent before You,
It is apparent and clear,
That if any of these
Openings would clog,
Or if any of these
Enclosures would seep,
I could not exist and live
In Your sight,
Not even for a moment.

So I'm grateful
And bless You
For healing me
In amazing ways.

> If you wish, you may wrap in the *tallit gadol* for *Shaḫarit* and lay *tefillin*.

## *N'shamah Sh'natata Bi*
### 'The Breath You Have Given Me'

My God, the breath
You have given me
Is pure and refreshing;
*You* create it, *You* form it,
*You* breathe it into me,
And *You* keep me
Breathing.

One day —
*You* will take it from me;
I will have breathed
My last breath
In this body,
And *You* will

Resuscitate me
To the life of the spirit.

With every breath
Still in me,
I thank You, my God,
God of my forebears,
Sustenance of all spirits,
Master of all that happens.

I worship *You—Yah*,
Who with each breath,
Gives me life anew.


*Birkhot ha-Torah*
'Blessings of the Torah'

You connect
Us with You
Through our awareness
Of Your *Torah*;
For this guidance,
We offer You
Our appreciation,
*Yah*, our God.

We ask that
We may find
Fervor and delight
In the words
Of Your teaching;
May we and our children
(And their children too)
Become intimate
With You,
And with pure intent,
Immerse ourselves
In Your *Torah*.

> *Barukh Attah Yah*

You mentor
Your people in *Torah*.

> *Barukh Attah Yah*

I offer You thanks,
Cosmic Majesty,
And worship You,
For selecting us
Among all nations
To reveal to us
The *Torah* meant for us.

> *Barukh Attah Yah*

You gift us continually
With Your *Torah*.

> If you wish, open to a
> passage of Torah at random
> with the intention of being
> guided to the words needed,
> looking on them with sacred
> eyes.


*Birkhot ha-Shaḥar*
'Blessings of the
Morning'

> *Barukh Attah Yah*

I offer You thanks,
Cosmic Majesty,
And worship You,
For giving me the gift
To discern the difference
Between darkness
And light.

### Barukh Attah Yah

I offer You thanks,
Cosmic Majesty,
And worship You,
For giving me
The gift of sight.

### Barukh Attah Yah

I offer You thanks,
Cosmic Majesty,
And worship You,
For giving freedom
Of movement
To my body.

### Barukh Attah Yah

I offer You thanks,
Cosmic Majesty,
And worship You,
For helping me
To stand upright.

### Barukh Attah Yah

I offer You thanks,
Cosmic Majesty,
And worship You,
For clothing my body
In warmth and protection.

### Barukh Attah Yah

I offer You thanks,
Cosmic Majesty,
And worship You,
For the firm ground
On which You place
And balance me.

### Barukh Attah Yah

I offer You thanks,
Cosmic Majesty,
And worship You,
For leading my steps
In the right direction.

### Barukh Attah Yah

I offer You thanks,
Cosmic Majesty,
And worship You,
For providing for
My needs.

### Barukh Attah Yah

I offer You thanks,
Cosmic Majesty,
And worship You,
For imbuing this
God-wrestler
With strength.

### Barukh Attah Yah

I offer You thanks,
Cosmic Majesty,
And worship You,
For making my soul bright
As I wrestle and dance
With You.

### Barukh Attah Yah

I offer You thanks,
Cosmic Majesty,
And worship You,
For taking my weariness
And giving me energy.

I offer You thanks,
Cosmic Majesty,
And worship You,
For shaping my life
In Your image.

*Barukh Attah Yah*

I offer You thanks,
Cosmic Majesty,
And worship You,
For giving me
The power to choose.

*Barukh Attah Yah*

I offer You thanks,
Cosmic Majesty,
And worship You,
For giving me
The privilege
To worship You as a Jew.

*Barukh Attah Yah*

I offer You thanks,
Cosmic Majesty,
And worship You,
For removing the last
Trace of sleep
From my eyes.

*Y'hi Ratzon*
'May it be Your Will'

And we ask
Your blessed help

To find that our habits
Follow Your *Torah*,
To make our desire
Seek Your *mitzvot*.

Do not allow negativity
To attract us,
But draw us
Toward goodness
And acts of
Loving-kindness;
Induce even our
selfishness
To serve Your ends;
Help us this day
To be generous,
Friendly and cheerful.

As we face You
And all who we may meet,
Keep us in Your grace,
And bless us.

*Barukh Attah Yah*

You are always
Generous to us,
Your people, Israel.
*Amen.*

*V'a'havta
L'rey'akha Kamokha*

'I accept upon myself
the command to
love my neighbor
as myself.'

## T'fillat ha-Yetzirah
'The Prayer of Feeling'

## Psalm 30

> A song of housewarming
> composed by David.

*Yah*, I acclaim You;
You set me free
So that my enemies
Cannot gloat
Over my troubles;
*Yah*, my God,
I plead with You,
And You heal me;
You lift me up
From the pit,
From the brink
Of the grave,
And bring me
Back to Life.

Join me in my song,
Fellow devotees!
Remembering
What is sacred,
Let us give thanks!

For a moment,
You were angry,
Then I felt life
And acceptance;
Though I fell asleep
Weeping,
I awoke
With song.

*Yah*, You make me
Firm as a mountain;
I thought I was safe,

That I would
Never stumble,
But when You
Hid Your face from me,
I panicked —
I called to You, *Yah!*
I pleaded with You,
*Adonai!*
What use is there
In my death?
To go down in ruin?
Can dust appreciate You?
Can it discern Your Truth?
*Yah!* Listen —
Be kind to me!
*Yah*, please help me;
You turned my grieving
Into a joyful dance,
You took my rags
And wrapped me
In happiness;
Now Your Glory
Is my song,
I won't hold back;
*Yah*, my God,
I will ever be grateful!

## Psalm 67

> A song for all the people
> of the planet.

God, bless us with grace!
Let Your loving Face
Shine upon us!
We want to get to know
*Your* ways here on Earth,
Seeing how Your
Help is given
To every group of people;

13

Oh, how the various
Peoples will thank You,
They will sing
And be grateful;
Many will be
Joyous and sing
When You set them
On the right path;
And the peoples
Will cheer You;
Oh how they
Will thank You;
All of them will sing
And be grateful,
The Earth will give
Of Her harvest;
Such blessings come
From God,
Yes, from our God!
Bless us, God;
All the ends of the Earth
Will esteem You!

*Barukh She'amar*
'Blessed One,
You Talked'

*Blessed One,*
*You talked*
*The Worlds into being;*
*What a Blessing You are!*
*Blessed One, Your Word*
*Makes for becoming;*
*What a blessing,*
*Your Name;*
*Blessed One,*
*You decree and sustain;*
*Blessed One,*
*All beginnings are Yours!*
*Blessed One,*
*Your Compassion*

*Enwombs the Earth;*
*Blessed One,*
*Your Caring is kind*
*To all creatures;*
*Blessed One,*
*You are generous*
*In rewarding those*
*Who respect*
*Your Creation;*
*Blessed One, ever alive,*
*Ever confirming existence;*
*Blessed One,*
*You make us free,*
*You rescue us!*
*When we hear Your Name*
*We offer blessing — Amen.*

> *Barukh attah Yah,*
> *Melekh m'hullal*
> *batishba̲hot*

*Blessed are You,* Yah,
*My Prince, lauded*
*With praise.*

## Psalm 100

> Usually omitted on Erev
> Yom Kippur, Erev Pesa̲h,
> and H̲ol ha-Moed Pesa̲h.

Sing a song of
Thanks to God;
Join the symphony
Of the Earth;
In your gratefulness,
Meet Him,
Voices echoing joy
In God's halls.

In giving thanks,
We engage Her blessings;
We meet His goodness,
Here and now,
Her encouragement
From generation-to-
Generation.

You are filled with joy
Serving God's purpose;
Sound your own song
As you do it;
Certain that God is Be-ing,
We know that we are
Brought forth from Her,
Both God's companions
And His flock.

Enter into God's Presence,
Singing your own song
In grateful appreciation.

Thank You, God,
You are all Blessing!
In this world,
You are goodness,
Yes, Grace Itself;
This is the trust
We bequeath
The next generation.

## Y'hi Kh'vod
'May the Glory'

Recite with special fervor.

*Yah!* Fill our world
With reflections of
Your nobility,
So You will find joy
In Your Creation;

We adore Your Name
In all circumstances.

Those who come
From the East,
And those who come
From the West,
Celebrate Your Name
In their own ways;
*Yah* transcends all
Cultural boundaries;
Her glory is in what
Concerns Heaven.

*Yah!* this is
Your Name forever;
*Yah* is the watchword
Each generation passes
To the next.

*Yah*, You have set
Your *Shekhinah,*
Your Presence
In the Universe,
Your domain
Encompasses
All there is.

So Heaven is glad,
Earth is happy,
All nations agree that
You are Sovereign.

*Yah!* You are now;
*Yah*, You were then;
*Yah*, You will be forever!

*Yah!* Your reign is Eternal;
Earth is Yours Alone;
No nation can claim Her.

*Yah*, You void
The designs of tyrants;

*Yah*, You block
Their schemes.

People brood
Over many desires;
*Yah*, it is Your design
That prevails.

What You design, *Yah*,
Lasts through all time,
What You propose
Works for generations.

You speak
And it becomes reality,
You command
And it comes into
Existence.

*Yah*, You chose Zion;
You wish to make
Your seat there.

*Yah*, You have
Singled out Jacob;
Israel is Your treasure.

*Yah*, You will not desert
Your people;
You will not forsake
Your heritage.

Because You are caring,
You will forgive sin;
You will not destroy,
But time and again,
You will subdue
Your wrath
And not let
Your fury rise;
*Yah!* Please help us,
Our Prince!

Answer us on the day
When we cry out!

## *Ashrei*
### 'Praiseworthy'

Dwelling in Your house
Is happiness,
But offering praise to You
Is better still, *selah!*

For those who
Are at home with You,
There is satisfaction;
And for those who
Have You as their God,
There is serenity.

Everyday I offer
You my praise
And remember
You in all that I do;
For You are
Truly magnificent,
And Your greatness is
Beyond all knowing.

Generation
After Generation
Tells its experience of You
To the next;
Splendid and Glorious
Is Your Name among us.

My God,
My only Sustenance!
I hold You above,
And remember You before
All that I do.

My delight
Is to speak of You;
While others tell
Of Your awesome Power,
I praise Your
Overwhelming Kindness;
You are Gentle and
Compassionate,
Patient and Caring
With me, always.

Indeed, You are
Good to all of us;
All that You have made
You hold in Your
Tenderness.

You fashioned us
To be Your devotees,
To bless You
And to speak of the honor
Of Your Realm,
To draw our energy
From Your Power;
We are the heralds
Of Your Uniqueness
And Your Majesty.

You embrace the
Universes;
Your authority
Flows through
And binds every
Generation.

You keep us from faltering
And help us up
When we stumble;
So we all look to You,
Hopeful,
Trusting in Your
Providence,

Guiding us
In the right moment
To what we really need.

You open Your hand
And each of us receives
What we truly desire.

You are a *Tzaddik*
In all Your ways,
A *Hasid*,
In all that You do!

You are close by
When we call on You,
Shaping our will
And our awareness,
Hearing our
Plaintive voices
With Your help.

You protect those
Who are Your lovers
And dissolve
The negativity
Of those who have
Gone astray.

I offer my mouth
To God's praise;
May all bodies of flesh
Bless Your holy Name
For as long as there is
Life on this world.


Psalm 146

*Halleluyah!*
Spirit of mine,
Praise *Yah!*

I will indeed praise *Yah*
With my life,
I will sing to God
With all my being;
I will not rely
On the mighty;
What can people do,
Who can't even
Help themselves?
When their spirits
Leave them,
They return to the dust,
All their schemes
Vanished.
Happy is the one
Who is helped
By Jacob's God,
Whose hope is
Entrusted to *Yah*,
The One Who makes
Heaven and Earth,
The ocean and
All that lives therein;
*Yah* is the One
Who is forever,
The standard of truth
And sincerity,
She seeks justice
For the oppressed
And gives food
To the starving;
*Yah* is the One
Who frees the
Imprisoned;
*Yah* gives sight
To the blind;
*Yah* uplifts the
Stooping one;
*Yah* loves the *Tzaddikim*;
*Yah* protects the converts,
Consoles the orphaned
And the widowed,

Confounds the way
Of the mean-spirited;
Please *Yah!* Zion's God!
Manifest Your rule
In the world!
For us and for our children
*Halleluyah!*

## Psalm 147

*Halleluyah!*
It is so good
To sing to our God,
And to make music
To accompany the lyrics.

*Yah* builds Jerusalem
By gathering Her scattered
God-wrestlers.

He makes the
Broken-hearted well
And soothes the hurt
Of their bruises.

Counting the stars
And naming them,
She creates
Each one of them.

Great is our Master,
And powerful
Beyond measure;
No one can describe
God's comprehension.

*Yah* encourages
The downtrodden,
But the insolent
He brings low.

Offer gratitude to *Yah!*
With the harp
Sing songs of celebration
To our God.

She covers the sky
With clouds,
Thus arranging rain
For the ground,
Making the hills
Sprout forth grass,
Giving the beasts
The food they need,
Even the young ravens,
Who cry out to be fed.

She is not impressed
By the stallion's
Powerful flanks,
Nor by the muscles
Of a man's thighs;
*Yah* welcomes those
Who respect Her,
Who long for Her grace;
Jerusalem! Zion!
Give praise to *Yah*,
Celebrate that
She is your God!
Because She strengthened
The bars of your gates
And blessed your children
In your midst;
Your borders
She set to hold peace
And satisfies you
With good nourishment.

When He decrees
Something for Earth,
His command is
Swiftly fulfilled;
Snow, like white wool

He sends down;
Frost, He scatters
Like sand;
He sends hail like crumbs;
No one can stand it
When He brings
On the cold;
Sending His word,
He melts them,
Blowing warm wind
The waters flow.

She imparts
Her words
To Jacob,
Her statutes
And judgments
To Israel;
*Alas,* She did not
Give the same words
To other nations;
The same judgments
She did not share
With them.
*Halleluyah!*


## Psalm 148

*Halleluyah!*
Applaud and cheer *Yah*
To the Heavens.

Praise Him,
The most sublime!
Angelic assembly,
Sing *hallel!*
Heaven's hosts, sing
*hallel!*
*Hallel,* too,
Sun and Moon,
*Hallel,* stars of light!

Jubilation from
The Heavens of Heavens!
From the streams
Of endless space
He has decreed
Your existence,
Praise God
And be grateful for life;
He fortified you
To last long,
Set a directive
That cannot be disobeyed;
*Hallel*, too, from Earth,
From dragons
And deep canyons,
Fire, hail, snow and fog,
Tempests and storms
Obeying His word;
Mountains, *hallel!*
And hills echo *hallel!*
Fruit trees and cedars
Sway their praise,
Wild and tame creatures,
Creepers and
Winged birds.

*Hallel* too from you,
Rulers of lands
And nations,
Officials and judges
Of the land;
Lads and lasses, *hallel!*
Elders and youths,
All of you,
Praise *Yah*'s Name;
His very Name
Is transcendent;
His glory is reflected
By Heaven and Earth.
Grand is the fate
Of His people,
His devout ones

In constant adoration;
*Halleluyah* those intimate
And close to Him,
You Children of Israel,
*Halleluyah!*


# Psalm 149

*Halleluyah!*
Sing a new song to *Yah*;
This is how
He is celebrated
Among the *Hasidim*;
Israel rejoices
In knowing its Maker,
Zion's children
Delight in their Prince;
Dancing, they chant
Her Name,
Making rhythm
With drums and strings;
*Yah* loves Her people;
The self-effacing
Can count on Her for help;
*Hasidim* savor
His awesome Presence;
Even on their bed,
They hum His praises;
They exalt God in
Inner speech.

Such praise
Is a potent blade,
Repelling antagonists,
Scolding bigots,
Immobilizing
Their commanders,
Arresting their agitators;
Rebuke them
As they deserve!

All this because
God's _Hasidim_
Give honor to Him
In splendor,
_Halleluyah!_


## Psalm 150

_Halleluyah_, Praise God!
In His sanctuary;
Praise Him powerfully
To the sky.

Praise Her for
Her potent acts;
Praise Her for Her
Generosity.

Praise Him
With trumpet sound;
Praise Him
With strings and harp.

Praise Her
With drum and dance;
Praise Her
With organ and flute.

Praise Him
With crashing cymbals;
Praise Him
With resonant cymbals;
Let all souls praise _Yah_,
_Halleluyah!_

*

Praise _Yah_, always,
_Amen, Amen_—
From Zion,

From Your dwelling
In Jerusalem,
We send our _Halleluyah;_
Praise to You, _Yah_,
Israel's God,
Who alone does
Amazing things;
May the glorious Presence
Governing
Numberless Worlds
Manifest in this world
In all magnificence—
_Amen, Amen._


## _Va-yevarekh David_
'And David Worshipped'

And David
Worshipped _Yah_
For all the crowd to see;
And David said:

I offer worship
To You, _Yah_;
Blessed are You, _Yah_,
God of Israel,
Our Parent,
Ruling countless Worlds.

All virtue is Yours:
_G'dulah_, _Hesed_, largesse,
_G'vurah_, power and law,
_Tiferet_, balance
And splendor,
_Netzah_, effectiveness,
And _Hod_, elegance;
For all that is
In Heaven and Earth
Is founded in _Yesod_,
The urge to live;
Yours, _Yah_, is majesty,

*Malkhut*, most sublime;
Abundance and honor
Are before You,
And You reign
Over them all;
In Your hand
Is force and might;
You can empower
And raise them up.

And, as of right now,
Our God, we thank You,
And sing to Your glory
With our utmost.

You, *Yah*, You alone
Have made the Heavens,
The Heavens
Beyond our Heaven,
All those that
Serve You there,
Earth and all that is on her,
The oceans and all
That they contain.

The Host of Heaven
Bow to You,
And You infuse
Them all with Life!

> At this point, you may want
> to dedicate a few coins for
> *tzedakah*, for charity.

You chose Abram,
You brought him out
Of Ur of the Chaldees,
You named him
Ab-raham,
And found his heart
Trustworthy enough
To make a covenant

With him;
On the day You saved us,
His children from
*Mitzraim*,
We saw how
You dealt
With *Mitzraim*
With superior force;
We, the people, saw it
And we put our faith
In You, *Yah*,
And in Moses,
Your servant.

We sang then
The great song,
And placed our
Trust in You
To bring us, to plant us
On the mountain
Sacred to You,
The Place You
Established
As a residence,
The sanctuary that
Your hands
Had set up for us.

*Yah* will reign there
Always!
*Yah* will reign there
Always!
On that day
*Yah* will be One,
And His Name
Will be One.

## Yishtabaḥ Shimkha
'Your Name be Praised'

Your Name
Be praised always,
Majestic One;
Powerful and
Gentle Source,
Making Heaven
And Earth sacred;
It is our pleasure
To dedicate
To You, our God,
And our parents' God,
Time and again:

Music and celebration,
Jubilation and symphony,
*Fortissimo*, anthem,
Victory march,
*Largo, forte*,
Paean and hymn,
*Sanctus* and *maestoso*,
*Laudo* and aria,
Celebrating Your
Divine reputation
In every realm.

We worship You, *Yah*,
Generous, great,
Regal One,
To Whom we
Offer all these.

God of our reverence,
Source of our wonder,
Fountain of all souls,
Author of all that happens,
Who delights in our
Music and chant,
Origin of unity,
You are the life that flows

Through all Worlds!
*Amen.*

---

### The Thirty-Two Mitzvot of the Heart

Reb Ahrele Roth, a"h, wrote a list of thirty-two *mitzvot* to be fulfilled in awareness, in the heart, and with the mouth. These may be used as a bridge to the next level of prayer.

My Creator!
May Your Name be praised:
With my mouth, brain and
Heart prepared, I am ready
To fulfill Your *mitzvot*.

You Who shape me:

1. Faith I place in You;
2. Oneness I affirm in You;
3. I am mindful of You;
4. I focus on Your vast greatness,
5. And on my own insignificance;
6. Thus do I turn back to You in *teshuvah*,
7. And am bashful in Your Presence;
8. I am awed by You,
9. And love You;
10. I accept the authority of Your *mitzvot*,
11. Find my joy in You,
12. And place my trust in You;
13. I deny all false gods and those in their service, rejecting all unfit thoughts that arise in my heart;
14. I give You my thanks,

15. And aim to hold You
    sacred;
16. I remember Jerusalem,
    Your House of Prayer
    for all Peoples,
17. And look to You, to
    redeem us and free our
    souls;
18. Amalek, I will blot out,
19. By loving my neighbor
    as myself,
20. And adhering to You in
    *d'veikut*,
21. Walking in Your ways;
22. Thus, will I make in me
    a holy space for You to
    be at home;
23. I long for Your intimacy
    and love,
24. And am energized to
    find You empowering
    my heart;
25. I affirm that Your
    actions are just,
26. And am mindful that
    You redeem us from
    *Mitzrayim*;
27. Therefore, I will not
    welcome in my
    awareness any thought
    that opposes faith in
    Your service, and in
    Your Torah;
28. I will not yield to pride;
29. I will not hate any fellow
    God-wrestler in my
    heart,
30. And I will give up all
    vindictiveness, and not
    consider myself flawless,
31. But remember that I
    caused You displeasure;
32. With all these, I intend
    not to forget Your
    Presence in my life.
    *Amen!*

Thus, may You be pleased,
Celestial Parent,
That by the merit
And the power
Of my making mention
Of these *mitzvot*
With my mouth,
There be stimulated
The energy of these *mitzvot*
In their Celestial root,
To draw down to me,
That high holy flow
That will shield my thoughts,
My voice and my words,
From all damage,
All taint, all dross and dirt.
And there be drawn to me
A flow that will make pure
My thoughts and heart,
My voice and words.
May all of them
Be surrendered
To You, be You praised,
To the end that I may merit
To be connected to You,
In *d'veikut* and love,
And to attain the fulfillment
Of Your *mitzvah*
To cleave to You.
Thus will I be privileged
To be an instrument
Of Your will,
A vehicle for the
Blessed *Shekhinah*
Of Your Glory.

Thus will the light in my soul
Not darken,
Nor will Your Divine spark
Be extinguished in me,
From now on and forever.
    *Amen!*

## T'fillat ha-B'riah
'The Prayer of Knowing'

> During the Ten Days of Penitence (before the High Holidays), Psalm 130 is said here.

### Psalm 130

From my
Innermost depths,
I call to You, *Yah!*
Hear what is in my voice,
Hear its pleading tone;
If You looked for sin, *Yah,*
*Oy!* Who could stand it?
And though You are
Generous with pardon,
We are often
Too scared to seek it;
Still, my very soul
Hopes for it, *Yah* —
So please send me
A kind word!

Among the watchers
For the dawn, *Yah,*
I long for Your Grace
To end my darkness;
Israel looks to You, *Yah,*
And You are so gracious,
Granting freedom to us all.

Yes! You will
Definitely
Free Israel
From all its sins.

## Barkhu
'Bless'

> At this point, your prayer becomes more inward.

I worship You,
*Yah*, Our God,
Cosmic Majesty;
For shaping light
And creating darkness,
For enlightening us
With compassion,
And renewing us
Each day in goodness.

My God, You
Have made us diverse,
Each with a
Unique wisdom,
And yet, we are all
Your Creation.

*Yah*, You are known
Over all the Earth,
And Your glory
Shines upon us
From the Heavens;
I am in awe of the vault
And the circumference
Of Your handiwork,
Of the luminaries
You spread before us.

The Messengers . . .
*Ofanim,*
Turning orbits
And planets;
*Hayyot,*
The supernal
constellations
Of the zodiac;

*Serafim,*
The blazing ones,
The galaxies;
All in concert,
Adoring You,
Sanctifying Your Name,
Chanting:

---

*Kadosh, Kadosh, Kadosh!*

---

*Holy, Holy, Holy are You*
God of Hosts;
The Earth is filled
With Your radiance.

You Are Alone,
Sacred Beyond-Limits,
But still we ask
That Your glory
Radiate to us
On the level
Where we live.

With Your benevolence,
You renew us each day,
Each moment,
The work of Creation.

Please, focus new light
On Zion,
And let us all receive
Its benefit.

---

*Barukh Attah Yah*

---

You shape the luminaries.

*Ahavat Olam*
'With an Eternal Love'

Ever and always
You have loved us
Into life;
You nourished us with
Kindness and abundance.

Holy One!
For the sake
Of Your Plan,
For Your honor,
And because
You taught
Our forebears
How to live
A life serving
Your purpose,
We ask You to
Share with us
In the same way.

God, gentle Parent,
We live in
Your caring embrace;
Make ours
An understanding heart,
Aware, careful
And effective;
Make real to us
What You speak
With so much love
In Your Torah.

May we always
See clearly
What You mean
To reveal;
May all our feelings
In *mitzvot*
Dwell harmoniously

In our hearts;
Focus all our hearts'
Longing
On the moment
When we stand
In Your Presence,
In both awe
And adoration.

May we never
Feel we have
To apologize for
Our love for You;
May Your Kindness
And Compassion
Be ever available to us.

Hurry with Your
Blessings and peace;
Lift the hold of
Estrangement from us,

> Gather the *tzitzit* together,
> and kiss them, as you say . . .

And gather us together
In this world,
So that we may feel
At home in it.

You can do this for us;
You have designed us all
For unique lives,
Bringing us close to You,
And we are grateful.

You are dear to us
And we are full of love
For You . . .

> *Barukh Attah Yah*

I worship You, *Yah,*
Who relates to us in love.

## *Sh'ma' Yisra'el*
### 'Listen'

> Say the *Sh'ma',* closing your
> eyes, covering them with
> your right hand.

## *Sh'ma' Israel*
## *Yah (Y-H-V-H)*
## *Eloheinu*
## *Yah (Y-H-V-H)*
## *Eḥad.*

Listen, Israel—

> Say your own name here.

*Yah* Who is, is our God,
*Yah* Who is, is One,
Unique, All there Is.

> *Barukh Shem K'vod*
> *Malkhuto l'Olam Va'ed*

Through time and space,
Your glory shines,
O Majestic One!

First Gate of the *Sh'ma'*

> I enter God's service.

Love *Yah*, your God,
With all your heart,

With all your soul,
And with all your might.

May these words
And values
I connect with
Your life today,
Be implanted
In your heart.

May they become
The conscious-norm
For your children;
Express them
In the intimacy
Of your home,
As you go out walking,
Pursuing your errands;
May they guide you
In your rest, in relaxation,
And energize you
With wakefulness
And productivity.

> Touch the place of the arm-
> *t'fillin*, directed at the heart,
> and say:

Bind them as a sign
On your arm,

> Touch the place of the head-
> *t'fillin*, directed at the mind,
> and say:

Let them be a beacon
Before your eyes,
Focusing your attention
And insight.

Inscribe them
On all your transitions,

On all your thresholds,
At home, and in
Your environment.

## Second Gate
## of the *Sh'ma'*

> I take upon myself the
> obligation of the *mitzvot*.

How good it will be
When you *really* listen
And hear the directions
I give you *today*
For loving *Yah*
Who is Your God,
Acting godly,
With all your
Heart's feeling,
And all your
Soul's inspiration.

*Then,* your earthly needs
Will be met
At the right time,
And the rains
Will descend
In their season;
You will reap
What you plant
For your delight
And health;
Your animals will have
Ample sustenance;
All of you will eat
And be content.

Be aware, watch out!
Don't let your cravings
Delude you;
Don't become alienated;

Don't let your cravings
Become your gods;
Don't debase yourself
Before them,
Because the God-sense
Within you
Will become distorted;
Heaven will be
Shut to you,
Grace will not descend,
And Earth will not yield
Her produce;
Your rushing
Will destroy you!
And Earth will not be able
To recover Her
Good balance
In which God's gifts
Manifest.

May these words,
These values of Mine
Reside in your
Heart-feelings
And soul-aspirations,

---

Touch the place of the arm-
*t'fillin*, directed at the heart,
and say:

---

Bind them as signs
On your arms,
Marking what you
produce,

---

Touch the place of the head-
*t'fillin*, directed at the mind,
and say:

---

Let them be a beacon
Before your eyes,

Guiding what you
Perceive.

Teach them to
Your children
So that they are
Instructed
In how to make
Their homes sacred,
In how to deal
With the traffic
Of life outside.

May these values
Of Mine reside
In your heart-feelings
And soul-aspirations;
When you are depressed,
And when you are elated.

Mark your entrances
And exits with them,
So you will be more
Aware.

Then, you and
Your children
And their children
Will live out on Earth
That Divine promise
Given to your ancestors,
To live heavenly days
Right here on this Earth.


Third Gate of the *Sh'ma'*

---

I intend to bring the *mitzvot*
to the world.

---

*Yah* Who Is said to Moses:

Speak, telling Israel to

Make *tzitzit*
On the corners
Of their garments,
So they will have
Generations
To follow them;
On each *tzizit*-tassel
Let them set
A sea-blue thread;
These *tzitzit* are
For your benefit!
Glance at them;
And in your seeing
Remember all the
Other directives of
*Yah* Who Is,
And act on them!
In this way
You will not be led astray,
Craving to see and want,
Prostituting yourself
For your cravings.

In this way
You will be mindful
And actualize
These directions
For becoming
Dedicated to your God;
To be aware *that*
I am *Yah* Who Is
Your God,
Who is the One
Who freed you
From oppression
In order to God you;
I am *Yah* Who Is

Your God,

*Emet*

That is the Truth.

\*

It is really true
That You, *Yah*,
Rescued us from
From *Mitzrayim*,
And freed us
From servitude.

Who is like You among
The powerful, *Yah?*
Who is like You,
Beaming holiness,
Whose feats are amazing?

*Barukh Attah Yah*

I worship You, *Yah*,

*Ga'al Yisra'el.*

Redeemer of Israel.

## T'fillat ha-Atzilut
'The Prayer of Being'

### Amidah
'Standing'

Say the *Amidah* silently or in a whisper. Remember your own needs and the needs of others at this time as well.

If you are pressed for time, use the short version of the *Amidah* on page 52 in the *Minhah* prayers.

Bow slightly at the phrase "*Barukh attah Yah . . .*" when it occurs in the *Amidah*.

*Barukh Attah Yah*

I worship You,
*Yah*, Our God,
God of our parents,
Abraham and Sarah,
Isaac and Rebecca,
Jacob, Leah, and Rachel;
Please remember
How they loved you;
Nurture us gently
With Your kindness;
We trust You will
Bring redemption
To us, their children,
Who continue to chant
Your holy Name,
And who love You still.

From Rosh ha-Shanah to Yom Kippur, add:

Remember us for life,
Sovereign of Life,
And inscribe us in
The Book of Life
For Your sake,
Living God.

Our Prince, our Helper,
Our Protector;
I worship You, *Yah*,
Shield of Avraham
And Sarah.

*Barukh Attah Yah
Magein Avrham u'fokeid
Sarah.*

Your power extends
Over all the Worlds;
You bring the dead to life
And all that is of help;

From Pesah through Shemini Atzeret:

You give us the dew

Between Shemini Atzeret and Pesah:

You blow the wind
And bring the waters
To the parched Earth
And its souls.

You sustain all life
With gentleness
And invigorate bodies
With Your flowing Mercy;

You support us in falling;
Heal us in sickness;
Free us from compulsion;
And keep faith with
Those now dead;
In Your might,
No one can compare
With You;
You deal out
Life and death,
Yet, in all this,
You make salvation grow.

> From Rosh ha-Shanah to
> Yom Kippur, add:
>
> Who is like You,
> Merciful Parent,
> Who remembers
> Creation for Life.

I worship You, *Yah*,
Who gives life to the dead.

> *Barukh Attah Yah*
> *M'hayeh ha-meitim.*

You are Holy,
Your Name is Sacred,
And those who
Aspire to be holy
Sing your *Halleluyah*
All day long.

I worship You, *Yah*,
God of Holiness.

> *Barukh Attah Yah*
> *ha-El ha-kadosh.*

I worship You, *Yah*,
And I pray for insight

And the right awareness ...

> Whisper the words that arise
> in your heart.

> *Barukh Attah Yah*
> *Honein ha-da'at.*

I worship You, *Yah*,
And I pray that we may
Harmonize with
Your Will ...

> Whisper the words that arise
> in your heart.

> *Barukh Attah Yah*
> *ha-rotzeh bi-t'shuvah.*

I worship You, *Yah*,
And I pray
For forgiveness ...

> Whisper the words that arise
> in your heart.

> *Barukh Attah Yah*
> *Hanun ha-marbeh*
> *lis'loah.*

I worship You, *Yah*,
And I pray for support
And redemption ...

> Whisper the words that arise
> in your heart.

> *Barukh Attah Yah*
> *Go'el Yisra'el.*

On a fast day, add:

Answer us *Yah*,
On this day of our fast;
Do not hide Your
Face from us;
Please comfort us
With Your kindness;
For You, *Yah*,
Are the One
Who responds
To Your people
In times of distress.

I worship You, *Yah*,
And I pray for healing ...

Whisper the words that arise
in your heart.

*Barukh Attah Yah*
*Rofei kol bassar*
*U'mafli' la'assot.*

I worship You, *Yah*,
And I pray for wholeness
In the ecology of
Our planet ...

Whisper the words that arise
in your heart.

*Barukh Attah Yah*
*M'varekh ha-shanim.*

I worship You, *Yah*,
And I pray for the
Ending of exile ...

Whisper the words that arise
in your heart.

*Barukh Attah Yah*
*M'kabbeitz nidhei*
*Ammo Yisra'el.*

I worship You, *Yah*,
And I pray for
A just society ...

Whisper the words that arise
in your heart.

*Barukh Attah Yah*
*Melekh ohev*
*Tzeddakah u'mishpat.*

I worship You, *Yah*,
And I pray for release
From the struggle
With negativity ...

Whisper the words that arise
in your heart.

*Barukh Attah Yah*
*Shoveir oi'vim*
*U'makhni'a zeidim.*

I worship You, *Yah*,
And I pray for
All righteous efforts
To succeed ...

Whisper the words that arise
in your heart.

*Barukh Attah Yah*
*Mish'an u'mivtah*
*La'tzaddikim.*

I worship You, *Yah*,
And I pray for Jerusalem,
Your city, and the
House of Prayer
For all Peoples …

Whisper the words that arise
in your heart.

*Barukh Attah Yah
Bonei Yerushalayim.*

I worship You, *Yah*,
And I pray for the
Rule of the Messiah …

Whisper the words that arise
in your heart.

*Barukh Attah Yah
Matz'mi'ah keren
Y'shu'ah.*

You hear our prayer
Compassionate Parent;
Accept our pleading with
Kindness and Grace.

I worship You, *Yah*,
And add my own concerns
Beyond what I have
Expressed before
And I trust that You
Will respond …

Whisper the words that arise
in your heart.

*Barukh Attah Yah
Sho'me'a t'fillah.*

Take pleasure, God,
In our prayer;
Teach us to encounter
Your Presence.

I worship You, *Yah*,
And may we merit to pray
In Your Temple in Zion …

Whisper the words that arise
in your heart.

*Barukh Attah Yah
Ha'mahazir Sh'khinnato
L'Tzion.*

On Rosh ha-Shanah and Hol
HaMoed, add:

Our God and God
Of our forebears,
Remember us
For deliverance,
Goodness, grace,
Kindness, compassion,
A good life and
Peace on this day of . . .

* Rosh Hodesh
* the festival of Matzot
* the festival of Sukkot

I worship You, *Yah*,
And am grateful for You,
And count our blessings ...

Whisper the words that arise
in your heart.

> *Barukh Attah Yah*
> *Ha'tov Shim'kha u'l'kha*
> *Na'eh l'hodot.*

On Ḥannukah or Purim, add:

And for the
Miraculous order,
For the salvation,
For the mighty deeds,
For the victories in battle,
For the wonders,
For the consolations,
For all that You did
For our forebears and us,
In their time, and in ours.

Followed by the appropriate prayer of the Ḥannukah or Purim holiday.

From Rosh ha-Shanah to Yom Kippur, add:

Please inscribe
All the children
Of Your covenant
For a good life.

I worship You, *Yah*,
And I pray for Peace ...

Whisper the words that arise in your heart.

> *Barukh Attah Yah*
> *Ha'mevarekh et ammo*
> *Yisra'el ba'shalom.*
> *Amein.*

Take a moment and search your conscience. If you find something in need of repair, make a commitment to do so, and ask for the grace to fulfill that *tikkun*.

# Yeridat ha-Shefa
## 'Bringing Down the Divine Influx'

### Taḥanun
'Supplication'

At this point, you may wish to recite Psalm 6 or Psalm 25 instead of *Taḥanun*. On days of joy and celebration, recite Psalm 15 instead of these. All of these are given below *Taḥanun*.

My God!
My soul is Your's,
My body is Your servant;
Take pity on what
You have created.

My soul is Your's,
My body is Your's;
God help us
For Your sake.

We come to
Honor You;
Help us in our struggle
For the sake of
Your honor.

You are kind
And compassionate;
Please, forgive us,
There is so much
To be forgiven.

Pardon us, Father,
Our errors are so great;
Forgive us, Royal Majesty,
Many are our mistakes.

Our God,
God of our parents,
Pardon our sins!
Erase our rebellions;
Let our failures not
Appear before You.

Mold our drives
To serve Your purposes;
Let our stubbornness
Be in Your service.

Refresh our conscience
To guard Your
Instructions;
Sensitize our hearts
To love You,
And to respect
Your reputation,
As Your Torah says—
*And* Yah, *Your God*
*Will sensitize*
*Your heart,*
*And the hearts*
*Of Your children*
*So that Your love*
*For God will be*
*Wholehearted,*
*And inspired*
*To make Your life*
*Meaningful.*

Dear God—
I approach You
From a desire
To serve You,
And yet,
There is no *Tzaddik*
Who can do only good
And not fail in it;
Please help me
With my moral life,
So that in every way
My attitude will be
Balanced and right;
To begin with,
Help me to forgive
Anyone who has
Frustrated or upset me,
Anyone who has
Sinned against me,
My body,
My possessions,
My reputation,
Or anything of mine,
Intentionally, or
Unintentionally,
Whether they
Schemed to do it,
Or were unaware,
Whether it was in
Thought, word,
Or deed,
Whether it was
In this incarnation
Or in another,
I completely forgive
Them all all
God-wrestlers:
Let no one be punished
On my account;
My God,
God of my parents,

May our prayers
Come before You;
Do not turn
Your attention
From our pleading;
We don't want to be
Impudent;
We don't want to be
Stubborn,
Claiming that we are
Righteous
And have not sinned;
Indeed,
We have sinned,
And our parents
Have sinned;
Help us, God,
Not to fail You again,
In what I here confess
To You ...

I beg You,
In Your great mercy,
Erase my sins,
But not by means
Of suffering
And illness.

May the words
Of my mouth,
And the meditation
Of my heart,
Be acceptable
To You, *Yah*,
My rock,
And my Redeemer;
I place my faith in You,
I place my trust in You,
I place my hope in You.

# Psalm 6

*Yah!* Please
Don't chide me
With Your displeasure,
Don't scold me
In Your wrath;
I need You
To show me kindness—
I am so miserable—
Heal me, *Yah!*
For my very bones ache.

I am deeply
Troubled within;
I ask You, *Yah!*
How long must
I endure this?
Please relent, *Yah*,
And for mercy's sake,
Pull me out and spare me.

How can I
Remember You
If I am dead
And gone down
To the pits?
Who will thank You
If I groan and
Am always worn out?

I sob upon
My bed at night
And my tears
Drench my mattress;
My eyes sting
From this frustration,
As if all my troubles
Wept them out.

Away with all you
Traffickers of filth
And pollution!
*Yah* has heard my crying,
*Yah* has listened
To my pleading,
*Yah* will fulfill my prayer;
Confusion and regret
Overtake you;
May shame finally
Bring you to your senses.

## Psalm 25

*Yah!* To You
I lift up my soul.

My God, I trust You;
Don't let me be shamed;
Don't let my detractors
Mock me.

All who place
Their hope in You
Will not be disgraced,
But shame will cling
To those who riot
Without cause.

Help me to
Know your ways;
Teach them to me.

Guide me
In Your Truth;
Teach me how to know
That You are the God
Of my salvation,
So that all day long
I may trust in You.

*Yah!* Recall
Your compassion
And Your kindness,
That precede all Creation.

Pay no heed
To the failings
And rebellion
Of my youth;
Only remember
Your good will for me,
*Yah!* For Your
Goodness' sake.

You are good and fair;
You can show the way
To the neglectful.

You guide the modest
In their judgments,
Teaching Your way
To the unassuming.

Those who witness to
And respect
Your covenant
Find that Your ways, *Yah*,
Are truly kind and real.

For Your sake, *Yah*,
Please pardon my flaws.
Though they are great.

When a person
So minds You, *Yah*,
You will teach them
The path to choose.

Such a person
Can sleep easily at night,
Knowing that
Their children
Will inherit the Earth.

You, *Yah*, impart
Your secrets
To the awakened ones,
You share Your
Mysteries with them.

My eyes are
Focused on You, *Yah*;
For You untangle me
From the trap.

Please, turn to me
With kindness,
For I am lonely
And wretched.

My troubles
Have opened my heart
And made space in it
For others;
Please, extricate me
From my despair.

See my struggle,
My heavy burden,
And forgive me
All my failings.

Do you see
How much I suffer,
How I am hated
For no reason?

Keep my soul safe
And free me;
Let me not be reviled
For my trust in You.

Because I do trust You,
Let simple directness
Protect me;
Please God!

Free all of Israel
From all their distress.

## Psalm 15

*Yah!* Who may be at
Home in Your tent?
Who may find sanctuary
On Your sacred mountain?
One who strides
With wholeness,
Acts with fairness,
Whose heart and words
Speak with honesty,
Not given to gossip,
Not hurting or shifting
Blame onto others.

Wary of his own motives,
He honors those
Who are respectful
Of God;
She will not stoop to lie
When she swears,
Even if it causes her loss;
He lends his money
Without interst,
And won't accept a bribe
To convict the innocent;
One who acts in this way
Will never waver.

\*

Dear God,
We delight
In the privilege
Of being created
For Your glory—

Not having to
Walk about in confusion;
Feeling the eternal life
You have implanted in us.

Open our hearts
To Your Torah;
Anchor Love and Awe
In our hearts for You;
Keep us from
Wasting our lives,
Causing discord
Around us.

We plead with You,
*Yah*, our God,
God of our Parents,
That we may be
Faithful to Your intent
In this life,
That we may live
To experience
The days of *Mashiah*,
And the life of the
World-to-Come.

Trusting in You, *Yah*,
Is actually *our* blessing;
So we will keep
Chanting in Your honor,
Offering our gratitude,
And not keeping silent.

*Yah*, You prove
Trustworthy;
*Yah*, You shaped
The Worlds;
Our trust
We can stake on this;
Knowing how
To call on You,
We can depend on

Your hearing us.

You've never abandoned
Those who sought
You, *Yah*;
This is true —
For You, *Yah*,
Do desire this,
In order that
Your justice prevail,
That Your Torah,
May become ever more
Compelling and strong.

## *Psalms for the Days of the Week*

*Sunday* – Psalm 24

*Yah*, the Earth
And her fullness
Are Yours,
The Cosmos
And all of its beings;
You founded the Earth
On the endless seas
Of time and space;
You set her by the streams
Of the great Flow.

*Yah*, who can rise
To Your summit?
Who can stand
In the presence
Of Your holiness?

One whose
Hands are clean,
And whose heart is pure,

Whose soul has no
False oaths on
Her conscience,
Who has not
Sworn to larceny—
Such a one will raise
A blessing from You, *Yah,*
Kindness and generosity
From You, her God,
And her help.

Such people
Are of a generation
That seeks You,
Like Ya'akov,
Seeking Your face,
*Selah!*

Open your mind
And your imagination!
Let the Gates of Eternity
Come into view!
The King of Glory
Will then appear;
Who is this
Glorious Sovereign?
*Yah Tzevaot—*
*The God of Diversity,*
The Queen of Glory!
*Yah!* Powerful and strong;
*Yah!* Ever victorious!

Open your mind
And your imagination!
Let the Gates of Eternity
Come into view!
The King of Glory
Will then appear;
Who is this
Glorious Sovereign?
*Yah Tzevaot—*
*The God of Diversity,*

The Queen of Glory!
*Selah!*


## *Monday* – Psalm 48

Here in God's city,
On this holy mountain,
God's vastness
And fame is so glorious;
This beautiful landscape,
Earth's palace of joy,
Mount Zion
North of Jerusalem,
The great city of royalty.

In her palaces,
God is known
In exaltation;
Here, the kings gathered
And came together;
*(If they came*
*As enemies …)*
Seeing it, they were
Overwhelmed with awe,
Like a woman in labor;
Trembling,
They took flight.

A storm You raised
From the East,
Shattering the
Cruisers of Tarshish;
All this we
Saw and heard
In God's city,
The seat of
*Yah—Tzevaot;*
May God keep it
Flourishing forever,
*Selah!*

In the midst
Of Your Temple,
We looked for
Your Grace, O God;
Your reputation
Is well deserved;
So we praise You
To the ends of the Earth;
Fairness and kindness
Issue from Your
Right hand;
Zion's mountain rejoices;
Judah's daughters
Celebrate Your justice.

Go 'round Zion,
Enfold her,
Take note of her towers,
Set your heart
On her strengths,
Raise her mansions high;
Then you will say
To generations yet to be:

*This is of God!*
*God eternal,*
*Who will guide us*
*Though death.*

## Tuesday – Psalm 82

God is present
To the godly gathering,
Presiding among those
Who administer judgment,
*(Warning them),*
"How much longer
Will you twist
Your verdicts,
Favoring the wicked?
*Selah!*

In your judging,
Consider the humbled
And the orphan;
Find justice for
The destitute
And the oppressed;
Assist the poor,
The down and out;
Save them from
The hands of the bullies.

Unknowing
And unaware you are—
You walk about
In the dark,
While the very
Foundations
Of the Earth are toppling.

I set up you to be judges,
To be like angels
Of the Most High;
But remember,
You too will die
Like everyone else,
Topple and fall
Like demoted princes;
Arise, O God!
Bring justice to the world!
You can bring order
To all the nations!

## Wednesday – Psalm 94

O God
Who settles scores!
Divine retribution!
Make Yourself known
As the Judge of the World;

Let the arrogant
Know Your justice!

*Yah!* How long
Will the wicked
And evil prosper?
Boasting of their malice,
They talk each other
Into still greater evil.

*Yah!* How they
Oppress Your people
And demean
Your legacy,
Murdering the
Widows and strangers,
Killing orphans!

They are deluded
In thinking that *Yah*
Cannot see this,
That the God of Jacob
Is unaware!
Boors—
Try to make sense!
Fools—
Will you ever get wise?

The One Who has
Planted ears upon us,
Can He not hear?
The One Who has
Shaped our eyes,
Can She not see?
He Who reproaches
The nations,
Does She not
Take them to task?
The One Who
Teaches awareness,
Is He not aware?

*Yah* knows
Our unworthy thoughts;
Blissful is the one
Whom You, *Yah*,
Take to task
And teach Your Torah,
Securing them
Against evil days,
Tiding them over until
Ruin overtakes
The wicked.

*Yah* will not
Forsake His people,
She will not
Abandon Her heritage;
Justice will return
To the courts,
Vindicating those
Of upright heart.

Will anyone
Stand with me
Against the wicked?
Who will stand up for me
Against the bullies?

Had *Yah* not helped me,
I would not have escaped
The silent tomb;
When my knees buckled,
Your Grace, *Yah*,
Held me up;
When I was overwhelmed
By disturbing thoughts . . .

*"How could You
Assist this malice?"*

I found comfort
And delight in my soul
From You!

Those who scoff
At laws and justice,
Who band together
Against the righteous
And shed pure blood
In savage meanness,
You paid back
For their crimes;
You, *Yah*, suppressed
Their evil deeds.

*Yah*—Is
My tower of strength,
The rock of my safety
At all times.

## *Thursday* – Psalm 81

Make music to God,
The Source of
Our strength;
Trumpet a fanfare
To Jacob's God—

*Louder, drum rolls,*
*Sweet violins and pipes!*

Greet the New Moon
With the *shofar!*
For even as the moon
Is hidden, we celebrate!

This is the imperative
For all Israel—
To prepared for judgment
By Jacob's God,
*(As on the day when,*
*Through God's*
*Judgment …)*
Joseph was empowered
To go out and rule Egypt,

Understanding a language
He had never learned!
And the heavy load
Was taken from his back,
No longer having to
Knead the clay.

You called on Me
When oppressed,
And I *(said God)*
Freed you!
In the thunder,
You heard
My secret message;
And later,
I tested you
At Meribah's springs—
*Selah!*

Listen, my people!
I witness this to you!
If only you would listen
To Me, Israel!

Don't cling
To a strange god;
Don't worship
An alien deity.

It is I, *Yah*,
Who took you up
From Egypt,
I Who fed you
And sated you to fullness;
But My people
Did not obey Me;
Israel did not desire Me
Enough to keep Me close;
I let them have their way,
Their heart's desire,
Allowed them to pursue
Their own devices!

*Oy!* If only My people
Would obey Me!
If only Israel
Would walk in My ways!
In a moment,
I would subdue their foes;
With My own hands,
I would repay them;
Those who loathe *Yah*,
And yet deny it,
Will have their rebuke;
*(But you who obey ...)*
I will feed
With the fat of grain,
And with satisfy
With honey from the rock!

## *Friday* – Psalm 93

Robed in dignity,
*Yah*—You rule us;
Girded with strength,
Donning intensity,
You arrayed the Cosmos
That it should not falter;
Your Throne was set-up
In the deepest past,
Before there was even
A world to rule.

The currents rush,
The mighty rivers roar,
And the ocean's breakers
Thunder and proclaim:
"*Yah!* is most powerful!
Your creation is witness
To sacred and eternal
Beauty of Your house.

On Rosh Ḥodesh, or any
other day in which you
appreciate God's hand in
nature, add:

## Psalm 104
### *Borkhi Nafshi*
'My Soul, Bless *Yah*'

O my soul—
Bless *Yah*, my God!
You have arrayed Yourself
In majesty and splendor—

*Wrapped in shawl of light,*
*Spreading out the heavens*
*Like a veil!*

Your upper chambers
Are roofed with water;
You ride the clouds
Of the wings of the
wind—

*The breezes You send*
*Are Your messengers,*
*The blazing flames,*
*Your servants!*

So soundly
You founded the Earth
To outlast time itself—

*But with the deeps*
*Of the abyss*
*You covered the mountains*
*As with a mantle of water!*

Then you roared,
Sounding Your thunder
Until they fled
And rushed away—

Mountains high
And valleys low,
Assuming their places!

You set them limits
They cannot pass;
Never again to cover
All the Earth —

*Springs flow into brooks,*
*And between mountains*
*They do snake!*

All the beasts
And wild of the field
Do drink there
And slake their thirst —

*By their shores*
*Dwell birds that soar,*
*Sounding their calls*
*Through leaf and reed!*

You drench the hills
With Your upper
Chambers;
From Your hands' produce
The Earth is filled —

*You grow fodder*
*For the tamed beasts,*
*And herbs with*
*Human labor,*
*To bring forth bread*
*From the Earth!*

Wine You provide
To warm and delight us,
Oil to soften and shine
Upon the face and skin,
Bread to sustain us —

*Even the trees*
*You sate with their sap;*
*The cedars You planted*
*On the Lebanon!*

There, the birds
Find their nesting;
There, the storks
Find their rest —

*Wild goats bound*
*Upon the heights,*
*And creatures hide*
*Behind the rocks!*

The Moon pulls
Tides and seasons;
The Sun knows
Where to set —

*You darken dusk to night;*
*The forest's night-life stirs!*

The big cats
Cry for their prey,
Praying to God
For their food —

*And return at*
*The rising of the Sun,*
*To crouch once more*
*In their lairs!*

While humans
Go out to their work,
To toil until the evening —

*How many things*
*You accomplish!*
*Making them all*
*With wisdom;*
*All the Earth*

*At your command!*

The sea is so vast,
Beyond all our grasping;
Countless are
Her creatures,
From the tiny krill
To the great whales—

*There go proud ships*
*And the Leviathan*
*You have shaped*
*To play and sport therein!*

They all rely
On Your care,
That You may always
Feed them well—

*You give to them,*
*And they receive it;*
*They are sated with*
*The gifts of Your hand!*

If You hide Your face,
They will panic;
If You recall their breath,
They will die
And return to dust—

*But You send your spirit,*
*And they are re-created;*
*Life on Earth is renewed!*

*Yah,* let Your glory,
Fill all time and space;
*Yah,* rejoice in all
That You do—

*You merely look*
*Upon the Earth*
*And she trembles;*

*You touch the hills*
*And they smoke!*

*Yah,* I live
Through Your song;
*Yah,* I am Your tune—

*May my speaking*
*Give You joy;*
*Yah, I am so happy!*

I so wish the world
Was without sin,
That all wickedness
Were gone—

*Yah, my soul, my breath,*
*Hallelu-Yah!*

From the beginning of Ellul until after Yom Kippur, we include:

## Psalm 27

*Yah,* You are
My light, my Savior;
Whom need I dread?

*Yah,* with You
As my protector,
Who can make me panic?

When bullies,
In hate,
Gang up on me,
Wanting to harass me,
To oppress
And terrorize me,
They stumble and fall.
Even if a gang

Surrounds me,
My heart is not
Weakened;
If a battle is joined
Around me,
My trust in You
Is firm.

Only one thing
Do I ask of You;
*Yah,* this alone
Do I seek:
I want to be
At home with You,
*Yah,* all the days
Of my life.

I want to delight
In seeing You,
When I come
To visit You
In Your Temple.

You hide me
In Your *sukkah*
On an foul day;
You conceal me
Unseen in Your tent
And also raise me
Beyond anyone's reach;
And now, as You
Hold my head high,
Despite the presence
Of my powerful foes,
I prepare to celebrate,
Singing and making
Music to You, *Yah!*

Listen, *Yah,*
To the sound
Of my cry,
And, being kind,

Answer me.

My heart has said:
I turn to seek You;
Your Presence
Is what I beg for!
Don't hide Your
Face from me;
Don't put me down,
You, who have
Been my helper;
Don't abandon me;
Don't forsake me,
God, my support!

Though father
And mother
Have left me,
You will hold me
Tight.

Please teach me
Your way,
And guide me
On the straight path.

Discourage those
Who defame me;
False witnesses
Stood up against me,
Belching out violence;
Don't let me
Become the victim
Of my foes.

*(I would not
Have survived)*
If I had not hoped
That I would yet see
*Yah*'s goodness alive
And fulfilled on Earth.

So, my friend,
Be sturdy!
And make strong
Your heart!
And keep hoping
In *Yah*.

## *Aleinu*
### 'Our Duty'

We rise to praise You,
Source of All,
Your generous work as
Creator of All;
You made us One
With all of Life
And help us to share
With all of Humanity;
You linked our fate
With all that lives,
And made our portion
With all in the world.

Some of us—
Like to worship You
As Emptiness and Void;
Some of us—
Want to worship You
As Sovereign of
Sovereigns;
We all consider You
Sacred and blessed.

We stand amazed
At the vault of the sky,
At the firmness of earth,
And deem You enthroned
In the Highest realms,
But also dwelling
Within us.

You are our God;
There is nothing else;
Your Truth
Is supreme;
Existence is
Nothing but You;
So Your Torah
Guides us—

*And you shall*
*Know today,*
*And take it to heart,*
*That Yah is God—*
*In Heaven above*
*And Earth below—*
*There is nothing else.*

*Yah*'s sovereignty extends
Throughout the Cosmos;
*Yah* will indeed govern
Over all there is;
On that Day,
*Yah* will be One
And Her Name
Will be *ONE*.

## *Kaddish*
### 'Sanctification'

If you are in mourning, and in the presence of a *minyan*, you may recite the *Kaddish*. The Mourner's *Kaddish* is recited for eleven months after the passing of a loved one, as well as on the death anniversary of a loved one.

*Yit_gaddal v'yit_kaddash*
*Sh'mei rabbah.*

*B'alma di_y'ra khir'utei.*

*V'yamlikh malkhu'tei,*
*V'yatz'mah purkanei*
*V'kareiv M'shihei.*
*B'ha_yei_khon*
*Uv'yo_mei_khon*

*Uv'ha_yei d'khol beit*
*Yis_ra'el,*
*Ba'a_galla*
*U'viz'man ka_riv.*
*V'im'ru—Amein.*

*Y'hei sh'mei rabbah*
*M'va_rakh*
*L'alam u'l'almei al_maya.*

*Yit_ba_rakh,*
*v'yish_ta_bah*
*V'yitpa'ar v'yit_romam*
*V'yitnassei*
*V'yit_had_dar v'it'aleh*
*V'yit'hallal*
*Sh'mei d'Kud_sha*
*B'rikh Hu.*

*L'eila min kol bir_kha_ta*
*V'shirah_ta tush'b'hah_ta*
*V'nehe'ma_ta,*
*Di_ami_ran b'alma*
*V'im'ru—Amein.*

*Y'hei shla_ma rab_ba*
*Min sh'ma_ya,*
*V'hayyim aleinu v'al*
*Kol Yis_ra'el.*
*V'im'ru—Amein.*

*Osseh shalom bim'romav,*
*Hu ya'asseh*
*Shalom aleinu,*

*V'al kol Yis ra'el.*
*V'al kol yosh'vei tei_vel*
*V'im'ru—Amein.*

If you are in mourning and do not have a *minyan*, you can recite the following words:

*El Malei Rahamim*
'Compassionate, Highest God'

Highest God!
Compassionate One,
Grant my beloved (—),
Whom You
Took to Yourself,
Gentle rest
Under Your
*Shekhinah*'s wings;
May the soul of my (—),
Who has gone
To other realms,
Find happiness and
Bask in the company
Of the holy and pure,
Who radiate light
Like the bright sky;
I will offer
As a *mitzvah*,
Alms to honor
(—) memory;
May the soul of (—)
The child of (—)
Find herself in the
Garden of Delight,
And may (—) remains
Be at peace,
And my (—'s) soul
Be united with
And bound up
In the chain
Of all Being;

Now you may say some of these blessings to those who have davvened with you, and to your own day.

May *El Shaddai*
Bless you,
Make you fruitful
And give you the increase
That will become
A source of harmony
For all people.

May *El*, the God
Of your forbears,
Help you!

May *Shaddai*,
Rain blessings on you
From above,
And from the
Deepest strata below;
Blessings of fertility
And nurture.

May God
Fulfill the blessing
To Abraham in you,
And in your loved ones;
When you are a stranger,
As Abraham
Was a stranger,
May you become at home
In that place, as he did.

May the blessings
Of your parents
(Jacob ...),

Swell and increase
Those of their parents,
(Isaac and Abraham ...),
To cap the desires
Of the ancient hills;
Be they upon
Your head (Joseph),
And surround the heads
Of your siblings.

God loves You—
God blesses you and
Gives you the increase;
God blesses your family,
Your land, your income,
And your holdings,
Right here on Earth,
As God promised
Your parents—
All peoples will bless you;
You and your possessions,
Will all prosper.

May God remove
All illness and pain,
All tensions and pressures
That you have known ...

The angel
Who redeemed me
From all that was corrupt,
Bless these children;
May my name, and
That of Abraham
And Isaac,
Be associated with theirs.

Be blessed in the city;
Be blessed in the country;

Blessed as you arrive;
Blessed as you are leaving.

May God decree
Blessing for you
In what you have stored up
For yourself through
The work of your hands
Here on Earth;
May this be your gift
From God;
May God open
Treasures for you
Of heavenly goodness,
Of earthly timeliness,
To succeed in
Your endeavors;

May you have
Good credit,
And never need it.

God be with you
And help you
At all times;
May you never
Have to feel shame
Or blame.

Go out in joy,
And arrive in peace;
May the mountains and
Hills sing you
On your way,
The trees in the meadows
Applaud your journey.

May you draw
Waters of joy
From the source
Of help;
May you live
To see the day
When you will be aware
Of God's ever-presence,

Helping you in your life;
O how we will celebrate
God's helpfulness
On that day!

So, say *L'hayyim!*
To one another;
To you, *Shalom!*
To your home, *Shalom!*
To all of yours, *Shalom!*

## *Ashrei*
### 'Praiseworthy'

Dwelling in Your house
Is happiness,
But offering praise to You
Is better still, *selah!*

For those who
Are at home with You,
There is satisfaction;
And for those who
Have You as their God,
There is serenity.

Everyday I offer
You my praise
And remember
You in all that I do;
For You are
Truly magnificent,
And Your greatness is
Beyond all knowing.

Generation
After generation
Tells its experience of You
To the next;
Splendid and Glorious
Is Your Name among us.

My God,
My only Sustenance!
I hold You above,
And remember You before

All that I do.

My delight
Is to speak of You;
While others tell
Of Your awesome Power,
I praise Your
Overwhelming Kindness;
You are Gentle and
Compassionate,
Patient and Caring
With me,
Always.

Indeed, You are
Good to all of us;
All that You have made
You hold in Your
Tenderness.

You fashioned us
To be Your devotees,
To bless You
And to speak of the honor
Of Your Realm,
To draw our energy
From Your Power;
We are the heralds
Of Your Uniqueness
And Your Majesty.

You embrace the
Universes;
Your authority
Flows through
And binds every
Generation.

You keep us from faltering
And help us up
When we stumble;

So we all look to You,
Hopeful,
Trusting in Your
Providence,
Guiding us
In the right moment
To what we really need.

You open Your hand
And each of us receives
What we truly desire.

You are a *Tzaddik*
In all Your ways,
A *Hasid*, in all
That You do!

You are close by
When we call on You,
Shaping our will
And our awareness,
Hearing our
Plaintive voices
With Your help.

You protect those
Who are Your lovers
And dissolve
The negativity
Of those who have
Gone astray.

I offer my mouth
To God's praise;
May all bodies of flesh
Bless Your holy Name
For as long as there is
Life on this world.

# A Concise *Amidah*

This short version of the Amidah has been adapted from the abridgement of J. F. Stern.

## *Havinenu*

*Yah*, help us
To understand
Your ways,
To sensitize
Our hearts,
With reverence
Everyday.

Forgive us,
With compassion,
Each and every sin,
That redemption
We may hope
One day
To win.

In Your caring,
Take our pain
And suffering away,
And satisfy us
With Your abundance,
We do humbly pray.

With Your
All-powerful hand,
Bring together
The scattered ones
To our own blessed land.

May justice
Be effective,
And righteousness
Prevail;

May evil plots
Be razed and fail;
May righteous efforts
Be well regarded,
And those who
Serve goodness,
Be justly rewarded;
May Your sacred city,
Be rebuilt with joy,
Your House of prayer
With all peoples be flll'd.

Then with a loud
And exultant voice,
Will the righteous,
O God of Israel,
Truly rejoice!

Let it be
Your divine will,
To quickly found
A messianic life
For all abound.

May the light of peace,
Brightly blaze,
As in reverence,
Your sacred Name
We praise.

For You do hear
The voice of prayer,
And are truly blessed!
This we declare.
*Amen.*

> Take a moment and search
> your conscience. If you find
> something in need of repair,
> make a commitment to do so,
> and ask for the grace to fulfill
> that *tikkun.*

*Aleinu*
'Our Duty'

We rise to praise You,
Source of All,
Your generous work as
Creator of All;
You made us One
With all of Life
And help us to share
With all of Humanity;
You linked our fate
With all that lives,
And made our portion
With all in the world.

Some of us—
Like to worship You
As Emptiness and Void;
Some of us—
Want to worship You
As Sovereign of
Sovereigns;
We all consider You
Sacred and blessed.

We stand amazed
At the vault of the sky,
At the firmness of earth,
And deem You enthroned
In the Highest realms,
But also dwelling
Within us.

You are our God;
There is nothing else;
Your Truth
Is supreme;
Existence is
Nothing but You;
So Your Torah
Guides us—

*And you shall*
*Know today,*
*And take it to heart,*
*That Yah is God—*
*In Heaven above*
*And Earth below—*
*There is nothing else.*

*Yah*'s sovereignty extends
Throughout the Cosmos;
*Yah* will indeed govern
Over all there is;
On that Day,
*Yah* will be One
And Her Name
Will be *ONE.*

# *Ma'ariv*
## The Evening Service

### *Barkhu*
'Bless'

> *Barukh Attah Yah,*
> *Eloheinu Melekh ha'olam*

I worship You,
*Yah*, Our God,
Cosmic Majesty;
For by Your Word,
Evenings descend;
And with Your Wisdom,
You open the gates
Of night's awareness.

With Understanding,
You vary the seasons
And teach us the
Rhythms of time,
The textures of the year;
You set the stars
And planets
In Heaven's vault
On the spheres
Of their appointed tasks.

You create
Day and night,
Rendering darkness
Into light,
And light
Into darkness;
You make our
Dawn and dusk;
As you bring
On the night,

You give us
Discernment
To know of its approach,
The descent of light
Into darkness.

> *Yah Tzeva'ot . . .*

Sustainer of Diversity
Is Your Name;
Living and present God,
May You always
Govern our lives.

> *Barukh Attah Yah,*
> *Ha'ma'ariv aravim*

I worship You, *Yah*,
For You cause
The gentle evening
To descend.

### *Ahavat Olam*
'With an Eternal Love'

Ever and always
You have loved us,
*Yah*, our God;
You impart Your
Torah and *mitzvot*
So that we may know
Reality and justice.

Therefore,
*Yah*, our God,
When we are
At rest for the night,
And when we rise
For the day,

We will make
Conversation
Of Your Torah
And rejoice
In Your *mitzvot*.

This is what we live for,
What keeps us going!

Day and night
We will ponder
Their meaning;
Just keep loving us
As we do so!

> *Barukh Attah Yah,*
> *Oheiv ammo Yisra'el.*

I worship You, *Yah*,
Who loves the people
Of Israel.

## *Sh'ma' Yisra'el*
### 'Listen'

> Say the *Sh'ma'*, closing your
> eyes, covering them with
> your right hand.

## *Sh'ma' Israel*
## *Yah (Y-H-V-H)*
## *Eloheinu*
## *Yah (Y-H-V-H)*
## *Ehad.*

Listen, Israel—

> Say your own name here.

*Yah* Who is, is our God,
*Yah* Who is, is One,
Unique, All there Is.

> *Barukh Shem K'vod*
> *Malkhuto*
> *l'Olam Va'ed*

Through time and space,
Your glory shines,
O Majestic One!

First Gate of the *Sh'ma'*

> I enter God's service.

Love *Yah*, your God,
With all your heart,
With all your soul,
And with all your might.

May these words
And values
I connect with
Your life today,
Be implanted
In your heart.

May they become
The conscious-norm
For your children;
Express them
In the intimacy
Of your home,
As you go out walking,
Pursuing your errands;
May they guide you
In your rest, in relaxation,
And energize you

With wakefulness
And productivity.

Bind them as a sign
On your arm,
Let them be a beacon
Before your eyes,
Focusing your attention
And insight.

Inscribe them
With your eyes
On all transitions,
On all thresholds,
At home, and
In your environment.

Second Gate
of the *Sh'ma'*

I take upon myself the
obligation of the *mitzvot*.

How good it will be
When you *really* listen
And hear the directions
I give you *today*
For loving *Yah*
Who is Your God,
Acting godly,
With all your
Heart's feeling,
And all your
Soul's inspiration.

*Then*, your earthly needs
Will be met
At the right time,

And the rains
Will descend
In their season;
You will reap
What you plant
For your delight
And health;
Your animals will have
Ample sustenance;
All of you will eat
And be content.

Be aware, watch out!
Don't let your cravings
Delude you;
Don't become alienated;
Don't let your cravings
Become your gods;
Don't debase yourself
Before them,
Because the God-sense
Within you
Will become distorted;
Heaven will be
Shut to you,
Grace will not descend,
And Earth will not yield
Her produce;
Your rushing
Will destroy you!
And Earth will not be able
To recover Her
Good balance
In which God's gifts
Manifest.

May these words,
These values of Mine
Reside in your
Heart-feelings
And soul-aspirations,
Bind them as signs

On your arms,
Marking what you
Produce,
Let them be a beacon
Before your eyes,
Guiding what you
perceive.

Teach them to
Your children
So that they are instructed
In how to make
Their homes sacred,
In how to deal
With the traffic
Of life outside.

May these values
Of Mine reside
In your heart-feelings
And soul-aspirations;

When you are depressed,
And when you are elated.

Mark your entrances
And exits with them,
So you will be more
Aware.

Then, you and
Your children
And their children
Will live out on Earth
That Divine promise
Given to your ancestors,
To live heavenly days
Right here on this Earth.

## Third Gate of the *Sh'ma'*

> I intend to bring the *mitzvot*
> to the world.

*Yah* Who Is said to Moses:

Speak, telling Israel to
Make *tzitzit*
On the corners
Of their garments,
So they will have
Generations
To follow them;
On each *tzizit*-tassel
Let them set
A sea-blue thread;
These *tzitzit* are
For your benefit!
Glance at them;
And in your seeing
Remember all the
Other directives of
*Yah* Who Is,
And act on them!
In this way
You will not be led astray,
Craving to see and want,
Prostituting yourself
For your cravings.

In this way
You will be mindful
And actualize
These directions
For becoming
Dedicated to your God;
To be aware *that*
I am *Yah* Who Is
Your God,

Who is the One
Who freed you
From oppression
In order to God you;
I am *Yah* Who Is
Your God,

---
*Emet*
---

That is the Truth.


*Emet V'emunah*
'Truth and Faith'

It is really true,
And we believe it . . .
That You are
Our redeemer;
We are awed when
We recall the miracles
And the help
You have given us;
You kept our spirits alive,
And often kept us
From stumbling;
You helped our people
And we accepted You
As our leader,
Vowing to follow
You always.

With Moses, Miriam,
And all Israel,
We sang to You ...

---
*Mi ka'mokha*
*Ba'eilim Yah,*
*Mi ka'mokha ne'dar*
*Ba'kodesh,*
*Nora' t'hillot 'osseh fele'.*
---

Who is like You among
The powerful, *Yah?*
Who is like You,
Beaming holiness,
Whose feats are amazing?

---
*Barukh Attah Yah*
---

I worship You, *Yah,*

---
*Ga'al Yisra'el.*
---

Redeemer of Israel.


*Hashkiveinu*
'Give us a Peaceful Rest'

Give us a peaceful rest,
And in the morning,
Awaken us to peace
And the good life.

We need You
To guide and assist us;
Protect us in the night;
Keep us in health
And safe from pitfalls;
Guard our coming
And our going
As You have
Always done.

---
*Barukh Attah Yah*
*Shomer et Ammo*
*Yisra'el la'ad*
---

I worship You, *Yah,*
Eternal protector
Of the people of Israel.

# Affirmations based on the *Amidah*

> You may wish to follow these kabbalistic affirmations of the *s'firot* which are based on the *Amidah* with your own personal affirmations:

I affirm the power
Of positive affirmations;
I affirm the *Shekhinah* —
Surrounding and
Blessing me;
I affirm the light-beings
Of God's service,
Who support
And guide me.

### *Avot*

I affirm the blessings
Of Abraham and Sarah
In my life.

### *T'hiyah*

I affirm the
Sacrifice of Isaac,
And God's power
Over my life
And my death.

### *K'dushah*

I affirm
God's holiness,
And my growth
Toward it.

### *Shover Oyvim*

I place myself
Under the protection
Of the *s'firah* of *Keter*,
Which will shield me
From all harm
And nullify it.

### *Atah Honen*

I invoke the
Influx of *Hokhmah*,
To align my intellect
With clarity and purpose,
To inspiration
And realization.

### *Hashiveinu*

I invoke the
Care of *Binah*
To lead me to the
Heart of Holiness.

### *S'lihah*

I invoke the
Abundance of *Hesed*,
To bring me
To atonement.

*Ge'ullah*

I invoke the
Power of *G'vurah*,
To see me through
All trouble
And lead me
To redemption.

*Refu'ah*

I place myself in
The compassionate heart
Of God's *Tiferet*,
And affirm the
Healing, balancing,
Integrative, and
Centering light
Within me.

*Brakhah, Mashiah,
Shekhinah*

I support myself on
The pillar of *Netzah*,
Channeling to me
All manner of blessings
And prosperity,
Which I place
At the disposal
Of the redeeming
*Mashiah*,
Unfolding to witness
The *Shekhinah's*
Residing in Zion.

*Kibbutz Galuyot,
Yerushalayim, Modim*

I support myself on
The pillar of *Hod*,
Making order in my life,
Gathering all the forces
From dispersion
And settling them
In blessed Jerusalem,
Where I offer my thanks
To God's Glory.

*Tzedakah U'mishpat,
Tzaddikim, Shalom*

I base myself
On the foundation
Of *Yesod*,
To act righteously
And justly;
To assist in every
Righteous effort
In the world,
And to become
Peaceful in the work
Of peace.

*Shome'a T'fillah*

I affirm that *Malkhut*,
The *Shekhinah*,
Is the one offering
These affirmations
In me...

And is attracting
The flow of blessings,
Which suffuses my life.
*Amen … Amen.*

---

Take a moment and search
your conscience. If you find
something in need of repair,
make a commitment to do so,
and ask for the grace to fulfill
that *tikkun*.

---

## *Aleinu*
### 'Our Duty'

We rise to praise You,
Source of All,
Your generous work as
Creator of All;
You made us One
With all of Life
And help us to share
With all of Humanity;
You linked our fate
With all that lives,
And made our portion
With all in the world.

Some of us—
Like to worship You
As Emptiness and Void;
Some of us—
Want to worship You
As Sovereign of
Sovereigns;
We all consider You
Sacred and blessed.

We stand amazed
At the vault of the sky,
At the firmness of earth,
And deem You enthroned
In the Highest realms,
But also dwelling
Within us.

You are our God;
There is nothing else;
Your Truth
Is supreme;
Existence is
Nothing but You;
So Your Torah
Guides us—

*And you shall*
*Know today,*
*And take it to heart,*
*That Yah is God—*
*In Heaven above*
*And Earth below—*
*There is nothing else.*

*Yah*'s sovereignty extends
Throughout the Cosmos;
*Yah* will indeed govern
Over all there is;
On that Day,
*Yah* will be One
And Her Name
Will be *ONE*.

## _Heshbon Ha'Nefesh_
### 'Examination of Conscience'

Before going to sleep, make a thorough examination of your conscience for the day. Check on your relationships, recalling whatever frustration or hurt was experienced during the day at the hands of others. Imagine them written on slips of paper; rip these up, one by one, forgiving fully those who have hurt you, as you say:

_Ribbono shel Olam,_
_Ha'reini moheil_

Master of the Universe,
I wish to forgive
Whoever has hurt
Or wronged me,
Whether deliberately
Or by accident,
Whether by
Word or deed,
In this incarnation
Or in previous ones;
I pray that no one be
Harmed on my account.

May it be Your Will,
_Yah_, my God,
God of my forbears,
That I err no more,
That I do not revert
To my old ways,
That I do not
Anger You anymore
By my actions;

May I no longer do
What is evil in Your sight.

Please, wipe clean
The negative impressions
That I have left
On others this day
With the Strength
Of Your Compassion,
But not through
Sickness or suffering.

May the words
Of my mouth,
And the prayers
Of my heart
Be acceptable
To You,
My Rock
And my Redeemer.

# Appendix

## That We Might Pray Well
### Elimelekh of Lizhensk

*Yah, our* God
God of our
Parents and forbears,
Who listens to
The cries of Israel,
*Your people,*
With an understanding
And compassionate ear;
Thus, we ask You
To hear our prayer now,
And grant us
Your great favor!

Please, open our hearts
And direct our thoughts;
Help our prayers to flow
Freely from our lips;
Incline Your ear to us
And hear how we,
*Your servants,*
Are seeking Your favor,
Crying out
With plaintive voices
And shattered spirits!

You are so kind,
So compassionate —
A God of infinite Mercy!
Please, forgive us —
Grant us pardon —
Atone for us, *Your people,*
The House of Israel!
However we have
Failed to do right,
Whatever we have
Done wrong —
Acting in wickedness
And rebellion against You —
*Let it be forgiven,*

*Pardoned and atoned*
*For us, Your people,*
*The House of Israel.*

Surely You know,
As nothing is
Hidden from You,
That it was not
Out of malice,
Or arrogant willfulness,
That we transgressed
Your Torah and *mitzvot;*
You know the fire
That burns in our bellies,
A fire without ceasing —
The *yetzer ha'ra* —
That selfish drive,
Which draws us into folly
And the vices of this world!

This *yetzer* confuses
Our awareness,
Even as we stand
Before You
In this moment,
Seeking to pray,
Pleading for life!
This *yetzer* incites us
And confuses our thoughts
With its base desires
And schemes;
How can we resist it?
Our awareness
Is so uncertain,
Our minds so unsteady
With troubles and anxiety,
With the thought
Of making a living
In difficult times,
Amidst oppression
Bearing down heavily
Upon us!

God of Compassion
And Kindness,
Fulfill what You

66

Have promised us,
What You promised
To Moses,
*Your faithful servant*,
When You said,
"I will favor
Whomever I will favor . . .
And I will be compassionate
With whomever
I will be compassionate."
This You have had
Our Sages tell us
Applies even to those
Who are not worthy,
For this is *Your* way . . .
To be kind
To both the good
And the bad.

It must be obvious to You
How troubled we are,
How hard our life is,
And what we must bear;
It is difficult for
Us to approach
And come near to You,
To serve You well,
To put our feelings
In harmony with Your Will
In all sincerity.

Oh heavenly Parent!
Can't You feel the pain
In our souls!
Please, please,
Arouse Your Mercy!
Let Your Kindness
Flow freely unto us,
Banishing and erasing
Our great attraction to evil;
Do not let our *yetzer ha'ra*
Have free reign in our
innards;
Don't let it seduce us
Into folly,
Deflecting us from

Your service!

May no evil
Schemes or desires
Arise in our hearts
While we are asleep or
awake,
Especially as we stand
In prayer before You,
Or as we are studying
Your holy Torah,
Or fulfilling Your *mitzvot*;
Let our thoughts be
Pure and clear,
Our awareness
Steady and strong,
Sincere and heart-filled,
As You would have it be.

Awaken in our hearts,
In the hearts of all of Israel,
*Your people*, the desire
To unify You
In all truth, to love, to serve
And bring You pleasure.

Root our faith in *You!*
Anchor it in our hearts
So that we cannot
Stray from it!

Remove all the barriers,
The obstacles in our
Own hearts
That separate us from You,
Our heavenly Parent!
Steady us, and help us
To keep our feet on Your
path,
To keep us from going
astray.

Please, do not forsake us;
Don't abandon us!
Keep us from
Being disgraced

Before You;
Be present to us
In the words of our prayer,
In the work of our hands
As they serve You,
In the thoughts of our hearts
As we remember of You.

Please, our heavenly Parent,
With Your abundant
Kindness,
Grant us this favor—
That our thoughts,
Our words and our deeds,
All of our motives
And our feelings,
Conscious and unconscious,
Manifest and hidden,
Be unified in truth
And sincerity,
Without a trace of self-
Deception.

Purify our hearts
And sanctify us;
Sprinkle us with
The waters of purification;
Wash us clean with
Your kindness and love;
Plant Your steadfast Love
And Awe in our hearts,
At all times and in all places,
As we go about our
Daily lives,
When we lie down
And when we rise up,
That Your Holy Spirit
May always be
Active and ardent
Within us,
That we may rely
On You always,
On Your great Love
And Awe.

Maybe we be

Securely anchored
In Your Written
And Oral Torah,
In the Torah
Which is manifest,
And in the Torah
Which is hidden;
In doing the *mitzvot*
May we unify
Your awesome Name.

Protect us from
All hypocrisy,
From pride,
From anger
And vindictiveness,
From tale-bearing
And depression;
Protect us from everything
Damaging to holiness
And the purity of our service
To You, whom we love.

Pour Your
*Ru'ah ha'kodesh* over us
That we may stay
Connected and close to You,
That our longing for You
May grow and increase;
Raise us up from rung-to-
rung
That we might approach
The rung of
Our holy forebears—
Abraham, Isaac
And Jacob—
May their merit protect us.

In this way,
You will always
Receive our prayer,
You will always answer us
When we pray
For anyone,
Be it a single person,
Or the entire people of Israel;

May You rejoice in us
And may Your glory
Be reflected in us!

May our prayers
Always bear fruit,
Being fulfilled above
And below;
Please, do not attend
To our flaws,
Especially the sins
Of our youth,
As David *ha-Melekh*,
Peace be upon him, said
"My youthful sins
And my rebellions
Do not keep
In Your memory"."

Please turn our sins
And petty rebellions
Into merit,
That there may
Flow to us
From the World
Of Repentance
The challenging call
To return to You,
Wholeheartedly,
And to repair all
That we have damaged
Of Your pure
And holy Names.

Rescue us from envy;
Let not jealousy arise
In our hearts;
Do not let not others
Be vindictive to us;
On the contrary,
Place appreciation
For the goodness of our
Fellow beings in our hearts;
Let us not seek to
Find fault with them;
May we speak to everyone

With civility and gentleness,
And let not hatred arise in us;
Strengthen us that we might
Love You more.

You know well
That the root
Of our intention
Is to bring You
Pleasure and joy,
Despite our distracted
Hearts and minds,
Which struggle to
Keep our *kavanah*
Focused on You;
Please, illuminate us
With the knowledge of
Your good Purpose;
This is what we ask of You—
All merciful God—
Please accept our prayer
In Compassion
And Benevolence.

*Amen—May this be
So willed by You.*

# The Thirteen Aspirations of Faith

## I.

My God, I aspire to perfect faith in Your Infinite Light, issuing from a Source beyond time and space, and which, longing for a dwelling-place in the Worlds below, compassionately contracts Her Radiant Glory in order to emanate, create, form, and effectuate all that exists in the Universe.

## II.

My God, I aspire to perfect faith in Your Oneness with all of Creation; a Oneness without a second; a Oneness that says, all that exists in the Universe is called into being according to Your Desire in every moment.

## III.

My God, I aspire to perfect faith in Your intent and purpose in Creation, that the Divine He may become known to us through Creation, the Divine She, that we may expand this awareness until the Worlds are filled with the consciousness of God, as the waters cover the sea.

## IV.

My God, I aspire to perfect faith in Your unfolding plan, in which all of us may come to constitute one consciously inter-connected and organic whole; that every living being may know that You are the One Who constantly causes their existence.

## V.

My God, I aspire to perfect faith in all the paths through which the Holy Spirit manifests and reveals to us; that all Your holy manifestations are as one with the Torah that was given at Sinai, though they are called by different names in time and space.

## VI.

My God, I aspire to perfect faith in the mission of Judaism as an organ of the collective being that comprises all existence; that through Your compassion on all creatures, it be revealed to all how integral each Message is to the health of all the species of our collective being.

## VII.

My God, I aspire to perfect faith in the reciprocity of Your Universe which takes our impressions, that everyone who does good with one's own life takes part in the fixing of the world, and that everyone who uses that life for negative purposes likewise participates in the destruction of the world, that every action has an impact on the rest of existence.

## VIII.

My God, I aspire to perfect faith in Your perfect judgment; that the amount of good in the Universe is greater than the amount of negativity, and that our entire movement through the chain of evolution is designed to bring about the fulfillment of Your Divine Intention.

## IX.

My God, I aspire to perfect faith in Your tradition that the deeds of the mothers and fathers inure to the benefit of the children, that the traditions passed on contain within them the seeds of the light of redemption.

## X.

My God, I aspire to perfect faith in Your compassion, that our prayers are heard and answered.

## XI.

My God, I aspire to perfect faith in Your Holy *Shekhinah*, Your Presence dwelling in our midst, that all who show kindness to living creatures also show kindness to You.

## XII.

My God, I aspire to perfect faith in Your continuity, that physical death does not terminate the existence of the soul, that there are innumerable Worlds in which the souls reside.

## XIII.

My God, I aspire to perfect faith in *tikkun olam*, the fixing of the World, and its becoming alive, possessing a consciousness and feeling, becoming a fitting vessel for the revelation of the Divine Will.

Made in United States
North Haven, CT
20 June 2023